The

Needlecraft

══ *Magazine* ══

book of

Embroidery
Stitches

*A Step-By-Step
Stitching Guide*

Rebecca Bradshaw

future
BOOKS

Dedication
This book is dedicated to Joanne Bradshaw
for being my big sister

First published in 1994 by
Future Books
A division of Future Publishing Limited
30 Monmouth Street, Bath BA1 2BW

Copyright © Future Publishing 1994

Designed by Paula Mabe
Illustrations by Patricia Cuss
Edited by Jennifer Dixon
Photography by Rob Scott

A catalogue record of this book is available from The British Library

Isbn: 1 85981 020 9

Printed and bound in the UK by Butler and Tanner

We take great care to ensure that what we print is accurate, but we
cannot accept liability for any mistakes or misprints.

Contents

Materials

Fabric

There are many different types of fabric available for embroidery. When choosing your fabric you should always consider its intended use and how much wear it will receive. An embroidered picture will have little wear but items such as clothing and table linen must be able to stand up to regular washing. You should always buy the best quality fabric that you can afford as this will increase the lifespan of your work.

Embroidery fabric can be split into three basic groups, all of which include various weights and levels of quality.

Plain Weave

Also known as 'common weave', these fabrics do not have a regular weave (that is an equal number of warp and weft threads). Plain weave fabrics are tightly woven, usually with a smooth surface. It is on this kind of fabric that most surface embroidery stitches are worked. It is available in many different weights, which range from fine voile to heavy tweed and denim. Other plain weave embroidery fabrics include cotton, linen, silk, calico, and synthetics. Equally popular are fabrics combining natural and synthetic fibres.

Evenweave

These fabrics are made with an equal number of warp and weft threads which create regularly-spaced holes between them. The fabrics are usually labelled with a number of holes per inch (HPI), although the higher count fabrics are sometimes described by the number of threads per inch (TPI).

Evenweave fabrics come in a wide range of sizes; some of the finer linens have 36 HPI, while the coarser binca fabrics may have only 6 HPI. The type of evenweave produced is governed by the way the fabrics are woven.

A single evenweave fabric, such as linen, is made from single strands of warp and weft threads, while Hardanger fabric is made from pairs of threads.

Aida and binca, the most common evenweave fabrics for counted thread embroidery, are woven with several warp and weft threads. Counted thread work, such as cross stitch, Hardanger and blackwork, is worked on evenweave fabric.

Materials

Surface Pattern

This group includes fabric which has a pattern already visible on the surface. The pattern can printed or woven in to provide a useful grid for your embroidery to follow.

Gingham fabric has uniform checks which are particularly useful for cross stitch, while spotted fabric is good for smocking, or any embroidery stitch which benefits from dotted guidelines. Ticking or any striped fabric is also extremely useful as the printed lines can be used horizontally or vertically to keep your stitching even.

Threads

There are many embroidery threads, differing in both type and quality. You should always think about how your finished embroidery will be used before you buy the thread. If it will receive a lot of wear and tear, you should use hard-wearing threads such as stranded cotton. However, if it is going to be a decorative piece, you can use finer threads such as the metallic and silk threads which cannot be cleaned. It is best to

check the label of the threads you intend to buy to make sure that you know how they should be cared for.

Another thing to bear in mind when choosing threads is how well they will cover the lines of your embroidery transfer, or the background fabric in the case of counted thread work. You may need to experiment to get the thickness you require but there are a lot of threads to choose from. These are the main varieties:

Stranded Cotton

This is a loosely twisted, six-strand thread. The strands can be separated so you can obtain different thicknesses by varying the number of strands in your needle.

One strand forms a fine line which is good for small details or outlines, while six strands used together produce a bold, heavy line. Alternatively, you can combine different colours in the needle for subtle shading or a variegated effect. Stranded cotton is available in a wide variety of colours, which makes it a very popular thread to use. It is most commonly sold in pure cotton but is also available in silk and rayon.

Coton Perlé

This is a twisted, two-ply thread which cannot be separated. Made from cotton, it has a slight sheen which can add interest to your work if used alongside other, more matt embroidery threads. It is available in three sizes – 3 (heavy), 5 (medium) and 8 (fine) – and can be bought in a wide variety of colours.

Coton à Broder

Similar in weight to coton perlé, this is a lightly twisted, single-strand thread. It does not give a shiny effect but it is available in many colours. In fact, coton à broder has been used to stitch all the examples in this book.

Silk Thread

Available in twisted or stranded varieties, this luxury thread is ideal for stitching on fine fabrics where extra quality is important.

Flower Thread

This is a soft, fine, single-strand thread which is available in a wide range of colours. It is often used in counted thread work as an alternative to stranded cotton.

Soft Cotton

This is a tightly twisted, five-ply thread which cannot be separated. It has a matt finish and is best for embroidering on heavier weight fabrics.

Crewel Wool

Used for fine embroidery and crewel work, this is a two-ply wool which cannot be separated. It is nearly the same weight as one strand of Persian wool and is available in many colours. Other shades can be created by combining different colours in the needle, although this technique is only suitable on heavier weight fabrics.

Persian Wool

This is a loosely twisted, three-strand, two-ply wool. Many colours are available and, again, more shades can be created by combining.

Metallic Threads

Available in many weights and textures, these threads are best reserved for special effects as they are not very hard wearing. Some threads, such as blending filaments, can be combined in the needle with other types of thread to give a slight sheen or sparkle, to your embroidery.

Materials

Needles

There are three different types of needles most commonly used for embroidery – crewel, chenille and tapestry.

When choosing a needle there are a few points to consider. The eye of the needle should be large enough for the thread to pass through easily without stripping, but if the eye is too large the thread will slip out.

It is best to keep a few different sizes of needle on hand when working with a type of thread you haven't used before. This way you can experiment with the sizes until you get exactly the right one.

The length of the needle should suit the type of work you are doing and should be either sharp or blunt-ended depending on the fabric and stitch you are using. Most surface embroidery requires a sharp-ended needle except for working weaving or whipping stitches that should not pierce the fabric. In counted thread embroidery a blunt-ended needle is used to slip easily through the holes in the fabric.

You must always replace your needle when it starts to turn black as it will no longer slip easily through the fabric. You will find that using metallic thread turns a needle black far more quickly due to the constant contact with harsh thread.

Embroidery needles have larger eyes than ordinary sewing needles so that they can accommodate thicker threads. All needles are graded by number – the lower the number, the thicker the shaft of the needle.

Crewel

This is a medium length, sharp-pointed needle. It is most suitable for fine and medium-weight embroidery on plain weave fabrics.

Chenille

Used for heavier-weight work, such as Candlewick Embroidery, this sharp-pointed needle has a larger eye than a crewel needle.

Tapestry

This is a blunt-ended, large-eyed needle. It is used for counted thread work and for weaving threads and whipping stitches through other embroidery stitches.

Hoops and Frames

There are many different types of hoops and frames available for embroidery but you should be guided by the size of the project you are stitching. It is often practical to have a few, different-sizes to hand so you can choose which fits best.

It is a good idea to use a hoop or frame for almost every kind of embroidery. You will find it much easier to produce work with a neat, even finish. Working in this way also helps prevent the fabric from distorting. This is particularly important with evenweaves which are far more flexible than plain weaves.

Frames are available as either hand-held or floor-standing models in a wide variety of sizes.

Embroidery Hoops

Hoops work by holding a section of the fabric taut between two rings.
Wooden – these have two rings, the outer one with an adjustable metal screw which is tightened once the fabric is between the rings.

Metal/plastic spring – an outer metal or plastic ring fits over an inner ring which is spring loaded to keep the fabric taut.

Embroidery Frames

Frames are designed to keep an entire piece of fabric taut rather than just a section.
Slate frame – the fabric is stretched between top and bottom rollers which are then tightened. The sides of the fabric are laced on to the sides of the frame.
Stretcher frame – four wooden slats join together to form a square or rectangle. The fabric is stretched around the slats then stapled into position.

Design Transfer Materials

Dressmakers' Carbon Paper

This paper is placed carbon-side-down on to the fabric and the design is transferred by the pressure on top from a blunt point or a tracing wheel.

Pounce

This is used for transferring designs by the 'prick and pounce' method.

Materials

Transfer Pencils

Your design is drawn on to paper with this pencil. The paper is placed face down on the fabric and ironed. The heat transfers the pencil image on to the fabric.

Dressmakers' Marking Pencils

These pencils can be used to draw straight on to the surface of the fabric. The embroidery is then worked over the lines. They do not smudge and simply wear away or are brushed off when you finish.

Iron-on Transfers

These transfers can be bought singly or in books. The design is printed in reverse so that it is the right way up when ironed on to the fabric. Most iron-on transfers do not wash out, so you should be aware that you will have to cover all the lines with your stitching.

Other materials

Masking Tape

This tape is for binding the edges of your fabric to prevent fraying. It is also useful for holding a design in place while you transfer it.

Cotton Tape

Binding your embroidery hoop with cotton tape will stop the fabric slipping as you work. It will also stop your hoop marking marks on the embroidery fabric.

Tape Measure

Flexible tape measures are best for measuring fabric.

Thimble

These may be made from plastic, metal, leather or wood and are used to protect your middle finger while stitching. It can take a little time to get used to stitching with a thimble.

Scissors

Large scissors are needed for cutting fabric. Never be tempted to cut paper with them as it will blunt them.

Small embroidery scissors are useful for snipping threads or trimming fabric.

Lighting

Always work in good light. If you do a lot of your stitching in the evening it is worth buying a spotlight fitted with a daylight bulb. This will help you to see colours clearly and will stop you from straining your eyes.

Techniques

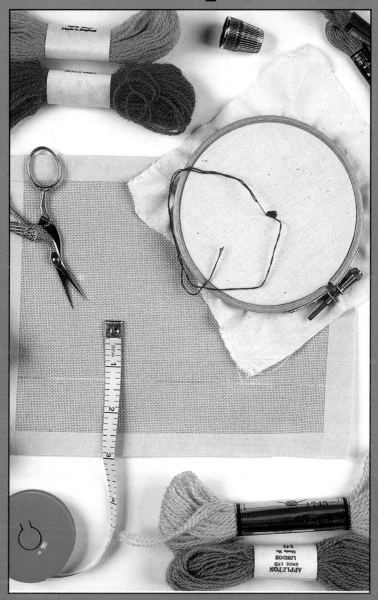

Preparing Fabric

Once you have chosen your design, fabric and threads, you can prepare to stitch. Calculate the amount of fabric you need by measuring your design and add an extra 2in (5cm) all way around. If your work is going to be framed, add 4in (10cm).

Cut out the fabric following the grain – this is especially important with evenweave fabrics as the threads are quite prominent. To prevent fraying or your thread catching as you work, you can use the quick and simple method of folding masking tape around the edges of the fabric. Alternatively, you can work blanket stitch or overcasting around the raw edges, or use the zig-zag line produced by a sewing machine.

Embroidery fabric can also be hemmed by hand or machine which gives a neat finish but takes time.

Transferring Designs

There are several ways of doing this. Choose the method you like to work with and the one that is most appropriate for your embroidery.

Iron-on Transfers

These are available ready-made, either singly or in books.

You can make your own transfers. Using a felt-tip pen, draw or trace your design on to a sheet of tracing paper. Turn the paper over and retrace the lines with an embroidery transfer pencil. This step is important as it ensures that the image is transferred on to the fabric the right way up.

To transfer the design, position the paper pencil-side-down on to your fabric, parallel with the straight of grain. Pin the paper down and press it with your iron on a fairly low setting. Press firmly all over the design, making sure that the transfer doesn't move or the design will be blurred.

Lift a corner of the paper to check if the design has been transferred. If it hasn't, increase the temperature of the iron slightly and press again.

Most transfers can be used more than once, although the impression will become a little fainter each time.

Dressmakers' Carbon

This is a coated kind of paper specially made for transferring designs. It works best on very smooth fabrics. Place the fabric right side up on a flat surface and tape it down. Pin the design on to the fabric, making sure that it is on the straight of grain. Slip a sheet of dressmakers' carbon between the design and the fabric, making sure that it is carbon-side down. Now draw along the design lines using a tracing wheel or a blunt point such as a knitting needle. The design will be transferred to the fabric ready to be stitched.

Prick and Pounce

This is a very old transfer method which is particularly useful for quilting and embroidery designs.

Place your design on top of a wad of fabric, such as a folded towel. Use a pin to make a series of small holes all the way along the design lines. You can do this with your sewing machine if you unthread the needle.

Place the 'pricked' design right side up on the fabric and pin it in position. The design is now transferred using 'pounce powder' or 'inking powder'. Use a small pad of felt to rub the powder gently over the holes. Remove the paper and

the design will be transferred. Finally, join up the dots with a dressmakers' pencil.

Marking Pencils

There are many different markers available. Whichever you choose, always test it on a spare piece of fabric first.

Water-erasable marker pens are useful as the completed stitching is simply immersed in cold water to make the pen lines disappear. You can also buy pens which fade gradually but these can only be used on short-term projects.

Dressmakers' chalk can be used to draw a design on to the fabric then brushed off. This method is best used for smaller projects as the chalk does wear away as you handle the fabric.

One of the simplest methods is to use an ordinary pencil. As long as you keep it sharp it should not show under the stitching. Also, the lines should wear away if you draw faintly.

Working with a Hoop or Frame

Most embroidery benefits from being worked in a hoop or frame. They keep the tension of the stitches even and give the stitching a much neater finish.

Hoops

Place the inner ring of the hoop under the fabric, directly below the area you want to stitch. Loosen the screw and place the outer ring over the top of the fabric and inner ring, pushing down firmly and evenly.

Your fabric should be 'drum tight' to work with. Tighten the screw and pull gently on the edges of the fabric beyond the hoop until you have achieved this. Also, it is important to make sure that the grain of the fabric is kept straight in both directions so that you are able to stitch evenly.

As you stitch, you may need to tighten up the fabric from time to time. This is done by loosening the screw slightly, gently pulling the edges of the fabric taut, then tightening the screw again.

If you want to protect your embroidery fabric from being marked by the hoop, which is especially important with fine fabrics, wrap cotton tape around the inner ring. Make sure that the tape overlaps as you wrap it round so that all the ring is covered. Fasten it

off securely at the end by stitching it into place.

If you are working with a particularly fine fabric, place a sheet of tissue paper over the area of the fabric you want to stitch on. Mount the fabric in the usual way with the tissue paper sandwiched between the fabric and the outer ring. Tear the tissue paper away to reveal your working area. This also keeps the rest the fabric pristine while you are stitching.

Frames

If you are using a rotating frame, you should hem your fabric all the way around the edge. Next stitch the top and bottom of the fabric to the tapes on the rollers using a small, strong backstitch – make sure that you position it centrally on the tapes. Attach the side arms to the frame. If you are mounting your fabric on a slate frame then you will need to lace the sides of the canvas to the arms.

If you use a stretcher frame, make sure the fabric is positioned centrally over the frame then staple the fabric around the bars and on to the back, making sure that the fabric is taut and 'drum' tight.

How to Stitch

You should not work with a piece of thread any longer than 18in (46cm) as greater lengths can separate or become knotted. If you are using a metallic thread, it is best not to cut your thread any longer than 12in (30.5cm) as this type of thread separates much more easily and then becomes difficult to work with.

Some threads have to be separated into the number of strands you wish to use. The best way to do this is to cut a length of thread then hold it gently between your thumb and forefinger about 2in (5cm) from one end. Take one strand and pull it gently. It will separate easily from the others in this way.

If you have to use more than one strand then you should always separate all the strands and recombine the number required. This method will make the strands lie flatter on the fabric when you stitch.

If you have difficulty threading your needle, you can use a needle threader. Alternatively, you can try folding one end of the thread over and pushing the fold through the eye of the needle. This method works especially well when using wool or thicker threads.

To begin your stitching, pull the needle and thread through the fabric leaving 1-2in (2.5-5cm) loose on the wrong side. Start stitching, making sure that the loose end is secured into the back of the stitches as you work.

Another starting method is to tie a knot in the end of your thread and pull the needle and thread through the fabric a short distance from where you want to start. Stitch over the end of the thread, then cut off the knot when you reach it.

When you have worked part of the design and want to start a new thread, weave the thread under the back of some of the existing stitches. You should also use this weaving method to finish a length of thread, but cut off the excess.

If the fabric you are stitching is likely to have a lot of wear it is important to start and finish all threads very securely so that they cannot come undone. Also, trim away all the loose ends as you go as they can give a very untidy effect by getting caught in subsequent stitching.

The embroidery stitches in this book are all explained with diagrams, photographs and instructions so all the information you need can be found later. However, a few general hints may be helpful.

Most stitches are worked using the stabbing method. This is when the needle and thread are taken through the fabric in one motion and back in another. This helps keep the tension of the stitches even and helps stop the fabric puckering.

However, there a few stitches, such as chain stitch and buttonhole stitch, which require the needle to be moved in one motion in and out of the fabric, to make a loop. You may find it easier to work these stitches without a hoop as long as you are careful to keep the tension even. This is often the case when working the buttonhole edges for cutwork.

When you are stitching over a transfer it is important to cover all the lines on the fabric, even if the transfer lines can be washed out.

If you need to move from one area of the fabric to another, you should not take the thread over too large a distance. This is because the thread can pucker the fabric and also it may be visible from the front of the work. If you do have to move more than 1in (2.5cm) you should finish off the thread and start a new one.

How to Finish your Embroidery

When you have completed all the stitching, wash your work in luke-warm water without detergent. If you have used a washable pen, or other marking pencil, carefully follow the manufacturer's instructions for removal. If colours bleed, keep rinsing until the water is clear.

Place a clean, fluffy towel on your ironing board and put your embroidery face down on top. Put a thin, clean cloth on top and press carefully. The thickness of the towel will ensure that you do not flatten your stitches. Iron the embroidered fabric carefully until it is dry, making sure that the iron is not too hot or you may scorch the fabric.

Take care if you have used metallic threads, as these may melt with the heat of the iron. Test a scrap first before you try ironing the stitched piece.

Outline Stitches

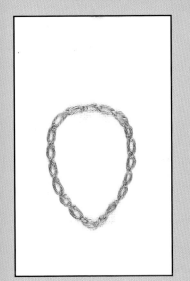

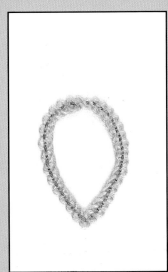

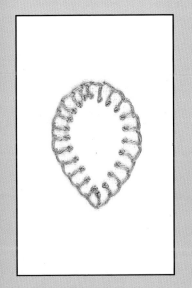

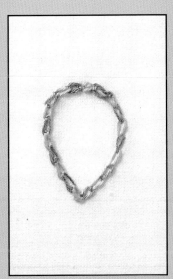

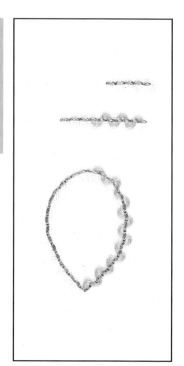

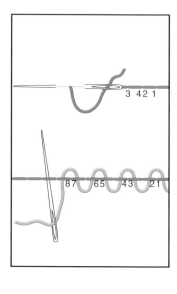

Working Instructions

Backstitch is one of the most versatile embroidery stitches. It forms a neat line which can be used alone or to outline other stitches. Threaded Backstitch is a more decorative variation.

Backstitch should be worked so that all the stitches are of the same length with no gaps between them. Bring the needle up at 1, down at 2, up at 3, down at 4, and so on. Continue stitching in this way, always working back on yourself.

Threaded Backstitch is worked by first stitching a line of Backstitch then lacing another thread through the stitches. Bring the needle up through a Backstitch at 1, down at 2, up at 3, down at 4, up at 5 and so on.

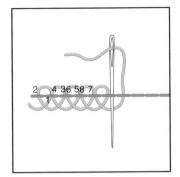

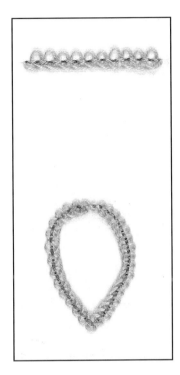

Working Instructions

Pekinese Stitch is a decorative outline stitch which is most effective when worked in two different colours. It can be used alone to form a line of any shape or worked around other stitches.

Pekinese Stitch is formed by first working a line of Backstitch then lacing another thread through it. Use a blunt-ended needle to loop under and over the stitches, making sure that you do not pierce the fabric. Working each loop from right to left, bring the needle under the Backstitch at 1 and down through the stitch on the left at 2. Pull the thread slowly to form a loop, then bring the needle up through 3, down through 4 and so on. It is important to keep all the loops the same size.

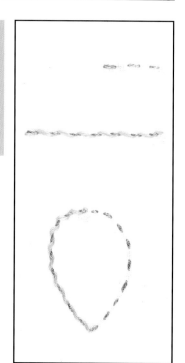

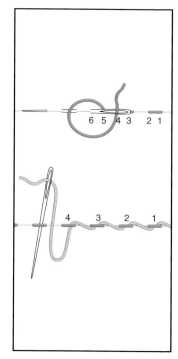

OUTLINE STITCHES

Working Instructions

Running Stitch is one of the most versatile and popular stitches. It can be used to outline, to pad before working another stitch, or even to strengthen the edge of a design for cutwork.

Running Stitches should all be of the same length. Bring the needle up at 1, down at 2, up at 3 and so on. The spaces between the stitches are usually the same length as the stitches themselves but you can vary the length of the spaces for effect.

Whipped Running Stitch is worked by first stitching a line of Running Stitches then working another thread, usually in a different colour, through the stitches. Always work the whipping stitches through the Running Stitch from top to bottom.

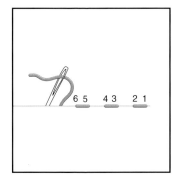

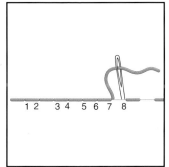

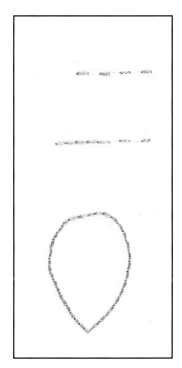

Working Instructions

Holbein Stitch is also known as Double Running Stitch as it is worked in two stages. It creates the same effect as Backstitch but gives a much neater appearance on the back of the work.

Holbein Stitch is traditionally used in blackwork and Assisi work and is also useful when stitching on Hardanger fabric as it does not pull the threads as much as Backstitch.

Work a line of running stitch for the first stage by bringing the needle up at 1, down at 2, up at 3, down at 4 and so on. To finish the stitch, work back along the line filling in the gaps by bringing the needle up at 1, down at 2, up at 3, down at 4 and so on.

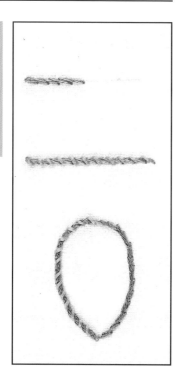

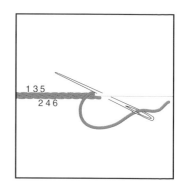

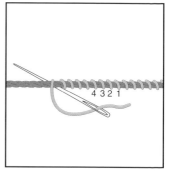

Working Instructions

Stem Stitch can be used to follow any shape and is particularly good for curved lines and emphasising other stitches. It forms a solid, raised line with a textured appearance.

Bring the needle up just above the design line at 1, down at 2 below the line and back up at 3. Continue in this way, always working back on yourself. Point 3 forms point 1 of the next stitch.

Whipped Stem Stitch is more decorative and gives a heavier line. The whipping stitches can be worked in a different colour for effect. Use a blunt-ended needle to work the whipping stitches over the line of Stem Stitch, always passing through the stitches from top to bottom to give an even appearance.

Portuguese Stem

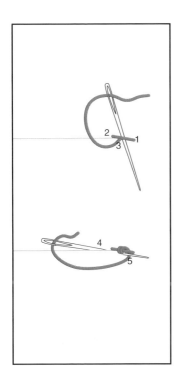

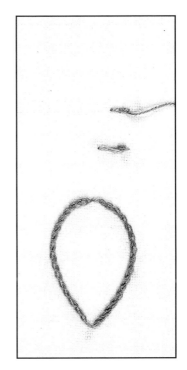

Working Instructions

Portuguese Stem Stitch forms a neat, knotted line which is heavier than Stem Stitch but equally versatile. It is good for adding detail to other stitches, especially if worked around filling stitches.

Bring the needle up at 1 and work a long stitch, pushing the needle into the fabric at 2. Bring the needle up again at the centre of the long stitch at 3, then take it over and under the stitch. Work another whipping stitch over and under the straight stitch, then push the needle down at 4 and up at 5 to make another stitch to the right of the first. Work two whipping stitches through this stitch in the same way as before. Continue in this way making sure that you keep the length of the stitches even.

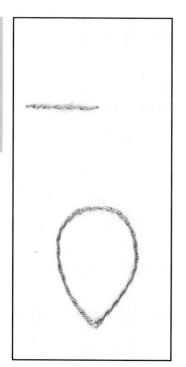

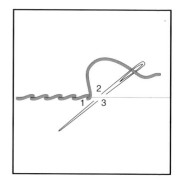

Working Instructions

Outline Stitch is similar to Stem Stitch in that it forms a fine, twisted line, which is ideal for outlining intricate shapes. It can be used for stitching straight lines and it is particularly well suited to working curves.

It is important to keep all the stitches the same length to achieve a uniform appearance, but it is an easy stitch to master. Bring the needle up slightly below the line of the design at point 1, then take it down at 2 just above the line and up again below the line at 3. Continue in this way along the line of the design. The needle should always be slanting to the left when you pull it through the fabric.

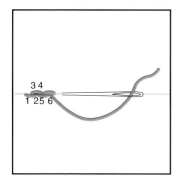

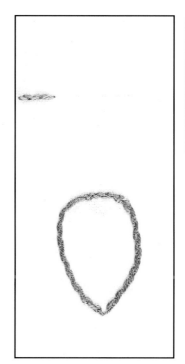

Working Instructions

Cable Stitch forms a neat line which is suitable for outlining any shape, especially curves. It is particularly good for emphasising natural details such as stems or small branches as it has as raised, textured appearance.

Work Cable Stitch from left to right by bringing the needle up through the fabric at 1, down at 2 and up at 3 in one movement. Push the needle down at 4, up at 5 and so on. It is important to keep the stitches the same length on both lines to give a neat, uniform appearance.

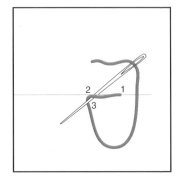

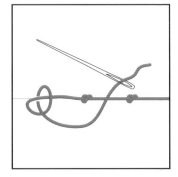

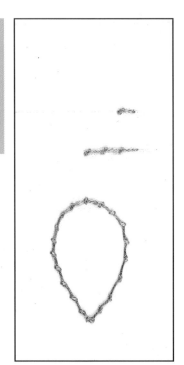

Working Instructions

Coral Stitch creates a narrow line which is made more interesting by small, evenly-spaced knots. It is very good for outlining shapes which have already been filled with another stitch as it gives a neat edge. Coral Stitch can also be used alone for linear detail such as stems or narrow borders.

Bring the needle up at 1 and down at 2, a short distance to the left. Bring it up again at 3, slanting the needle slightly without pulling it through the fabric. Loop the thread over the needle from top to bottom and pull it through the fabric slowly to form a knot. You will find it easier to make neat knots if you pull the thread slowly and ease the knot down on to the surface of the fabric.

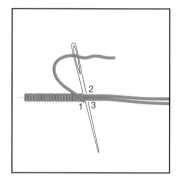

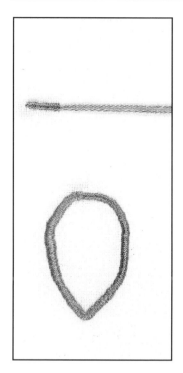

Working Instructions

Overcast Stitch gives a neat, raised line which can be used to outline any shape as it follows curves easily. It is good for fine, detailed lines such as those used for the letters of the alphabet.

Overcast Stitch is formed from two threads laid on the surface of the fabric which are manipulated into the required shape and held in place with small stitches. Bring two threads up through the fabric and leave them loose (make sure they are long enough to cover the whole length of the line to be stitched). Using another thread, work a series of vertical stitches over the threads. Bring the needle up at 1 below the loose threads, push it down at 2 and bring it up again at 3 below the threads once more.

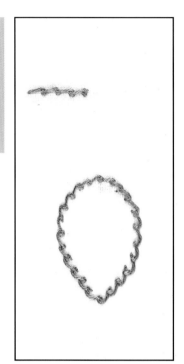

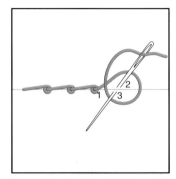

Working Instructions

Scroll Stitch is one of the most attractive, yet simple outline stitches. It is best used in decorative work as it forms a pretty, textured line. It curves easily and can be used for working around shapes already filled with another stitch. Scroll Stitch is especially good for stitching monograms.

Scroll Stitch is worked from left to right along the design line. Bring the needle up at 1, down at 2 and up at 3 with the needle slanting backwards, but do not pull it all the way through the fabric. Loop the thread around the needle, then pull it through the fabric gently to make a neat knot. All the stitches should be of equal length with the knots evenly spaced.

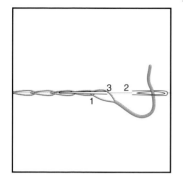

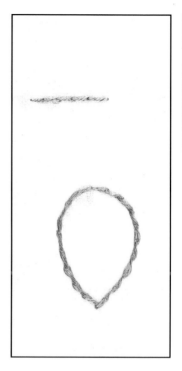

Working Instructions

Split Stitch gives a neat outline to any shape but can also be used to fill areas if worked in close rows. It is very similar in appearance to Chain Stitch as the thread is split to form small chain 'links'. It is best to use a loosely twisted thread such as crewel wool as it is easier to split. You should also use a sharp needle to split the thread neatly.

Bring the needle up at 1, down at 2 and up at 3 but do not pull it all the way through the fabric. Pull the needle up through the centre of the thread to split it, then carry on pulling it up through the fabric and thread. Work the whole outline in this way making sure you always split the thread in the centre to form even stitches.

OUTLINE STITCHES

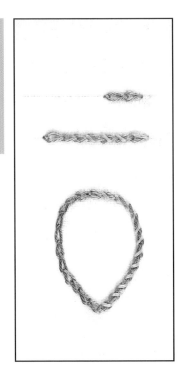

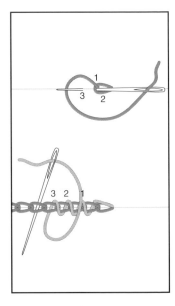

Working Instructions

Chain Stitch works well as a decorative outline as it curves easily and looks particularly effective stitched in spirals.

Work from right to left bringing the needle up at 1, down at 2 and up at 3, making sure that the thread is under the needle. Pull the needle through slowly to form a neat loop – do not pull too tightly or the 'chain' effect will be lost.

Whipped Chain Stitch creates a more raised line than ordinary Chain Stitch. First stitch a line of Chain Stitches then use another thread, probably in a different colour, to work through the stitches without piercing the fabric. Work the whipping stitches from top to bottom to give an even appearance.

Chequered Chain

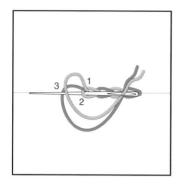

Working Instructions

Chequered Chain Stitch is a more decorative variation of Chain Stitch. It forms alternate coloured loops as it is worked with two different coloured threads in the needle.

Chequered Chain Stitch is worked in the same way as Chain Stitch by bringing the needle up at 1, down at 2 and up again at 3 keeping the thread under the needle. The difference is that you only put one of the threads under the needle then, when you work the next chain link, you put the other colour of thread under the needle. You can vary this stitch by working two stitches in one colour then two in the other, or any combination you choose.

Twisted Chain

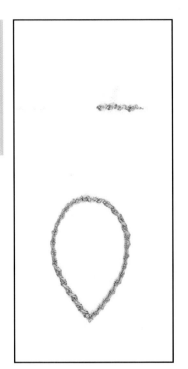

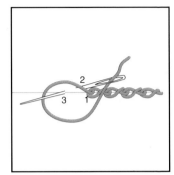

Working Instructions

Twisted Chain Stitch forms a narrow, raised line which is very attractive when worked in straight lines or around curves. It is good for outlining shapes or linear detail in pictorial work. It does not work as well for filling shapes in rows as it is not easy to cover the background fabric.

Work by bringing the needle up at 1, down at 2 and up at 3 to make a slanted stitch but do not pull the needle through the fabric. Twist the thread around the needle from top to bottom, then pull the needle through the fabric to make one chain link. Continue working along the line of the design in this way. Make the stitches quite short and all the same length to achieve a neat appearance.

Heavy Chain

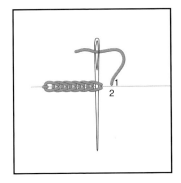

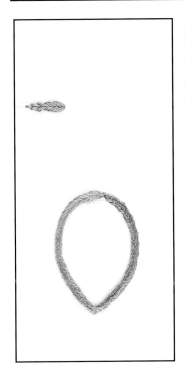

Working Instructions

Heavy Chain Stitch forms a flat, broad outline which is both effective and easy to work. It is good for pictorial detail wherever a heavy outline is required.

To start, work a short horizontal stitch on the design line. Bring the needle up a little further along the line, thread it under the straight stitch, without piercing the fabric, and push it back down where the thread emerged to make a small loop. To work the rest of the stitch bring the needle up at 1, through the loop from top to bottom then down at 2 where the thread emerged. You should make sure that you do not pull the thread too tightly and also that the fabric does not show through the stitches.

Cable Chain

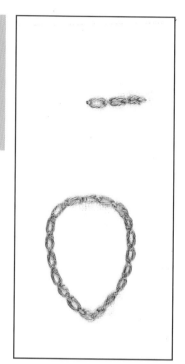

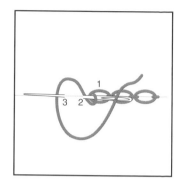

Working Instructions

Cable Chain Stitch is a very attractive stitch which is a variation of Chain Stitch with additional short stitches. It is very good for outlining curved shapes and can be used for decorative borders or abstract patterns.

To work Cable Chain Stitch bring the needle up at 1 and twist the thread around the needle, over then under. In one movement push the needle back down a short distance away at 2 and bring it up again at 3, with the thread under the needle. It is important that you make all the short stitches the same size and all the chain stitches the same size for a uniform appearance. Make sure that you do not pull the loops too tightly.

Buttonhole

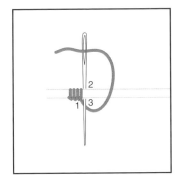

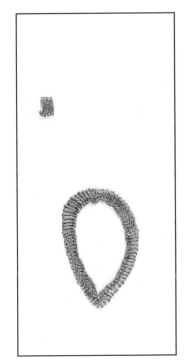

Working Instructions

Buttonhole Stitch is one of the most popular embroidery stitches. It creates a neat, solid line most suitable for finishing raw edges of fabric. It is commonly used in cutwork and Richelieu work for edging areas of fabric which are then cut away. Buttonhole Stitch is also good for outlining small, decorative motifs.

In one movement bring the needle up at 1, down at 2 and up again at 3, keeping the thread under the needle. The vertical stitches should all be of the same length and worked so closely together that none of the fabric can be seen underneath. You may find that it helps to draw two parallel lines on to the fabric as a guide to keep your stitches the same length.

Tailors

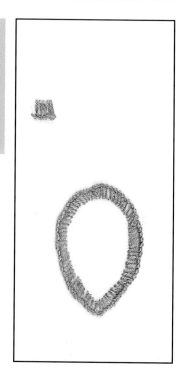

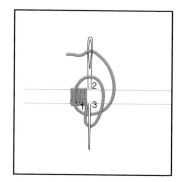

Working Instructions

Tailors Buttonhole Stitch is similar to Buttonhole Stitch in appearance but the edge is more raised. It is a very hard-wearing stitch mostly used for preventing fabric edges from fraying and being pulled out of shape. It is particularly useful when working with thicker fabrics. It can also be used for decorative work as you can use it to outline any shape, even curves.

This stitch is worked by bringing the needle up at 1, down at 2 then up at 3, without pulling the needle through the fabric. Wind the thread around the needle twice and pull gently through the fabric to form a neat knot at the bottom edge. The stitches should lie close together with no background fabric showing through.

Blanket

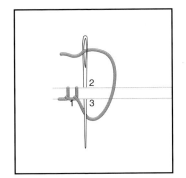

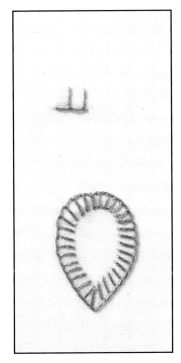

Working Instructions

Blanket Stitch makes a decorative outline which can also be used as a border stitch. As its name suggests, it was traditionally used to edge blankets to prevent fraying. This stitch is also used in appliqué to attach fabric shapes to the base material.

Work by bringing the needle up at 1, down at 2 and up at 3 with the thread under the needle. Gently pull the needle through to form a neat loop. The vertical stitches should all be evenly spaced and of the same length. You may find it helps to draw two parallel lines on to the fabric as a guide.

For a different effect try varying the length of the vertical stitches, alternating between long and short ones.

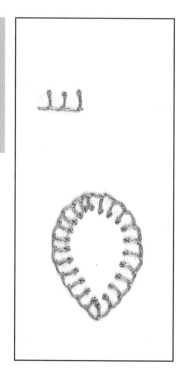

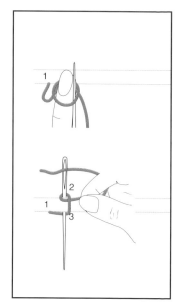

Working Instructions

Knotted Blanket Stitch is also known as Knotted Buttonhole
Stitch as the two are worked in the same way, only the spacing of
the stitches is varied (wider for former and close together for the
latter). It can be used as a decorative outline stitch for straight
lines or curves as it forms an attractive edging on both sides.

Bring the needle up at 1, then make a loop of thread around
your finger from right to left. Push the needle up through this loop
over your fingernail. Keeping the loop on the needle, remove your
finger and push the needle down at 2 and up again at 3. Before
you pull the needle all the way through the fabric, tighten the knot
and hold it in place while you complete the stitch.

Border Stitches

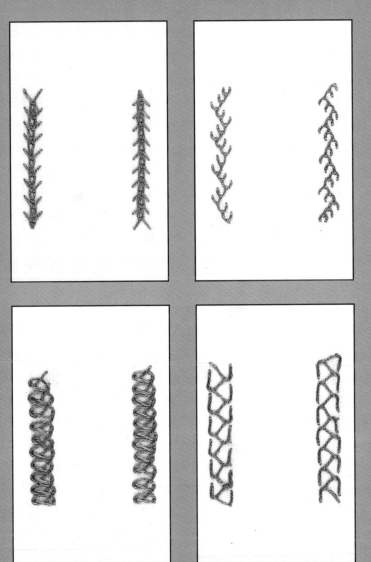

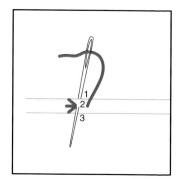

Working Instructions

Fern Stitch is a versatile, decorative stitch which can be used for straight or gently curved lines. It is effective as a border or it can be used to create branched lines suitable for depicting flower stems, leaves and trees. Draw two parallel lines on to the fabric to help keep all your stitches an equal length.

Each Fern Stitch is made up of three small stitches. Bring the needle up at a central point between the guidelines and push it down at 1. Bring it up at 2, down at the centre point, up at 3 and down at the centre point once again to complete the stitch. Each subsequent Fern Stitch should touch the centre stitch of the last.

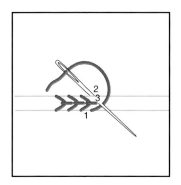

Working Instructions

Fly Stitch is similar in appearance to Fern Stitch but it is worked in a different, more open way. This versatile stitch can be used in rows to give a decorative border or columns for a totally different look. Fly Stitch can also be used as an isolated stitch worked randomly across a design.

Bring the needle up on the lower line at 1, then down at 2 without pulling the needle through the fabric. Bring the needle up again at 3, over the thread of the first stitch, and pull it through. Make a short, horizontal stitch to secure the 'V' shape. This sequence forms one Fly Stitch. If you are working in lines, place the stitches side by side or below each other.

Closed Buttonhole

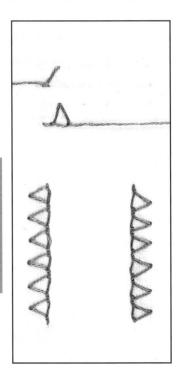

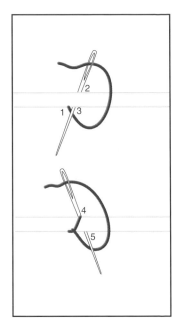

Working Instructions

Closed Buttonhole Stitch provides an excellent border. It can be used on the edge of fabric to prevent fraying or decoratively for pictorial work. It is most appropriate for straight lines and very gentle curves – the effect is lost if the stitch is made to curve too sharply. Draw two parallel lines on to the fabric to help keep all your stitches the same size.

Bring the needle up at 1, down at 2 and up at 3, keeping the thread under the needle. Push the needle down again at 4, in the same hole as 2, then bring it up again at 5 with the thread under the needle. Continue working the stitches in the same way to form small triangles along the line.

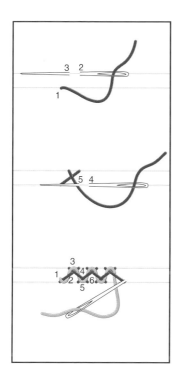

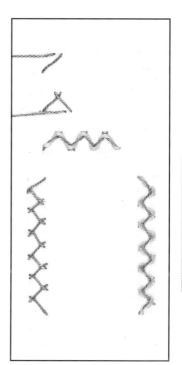

Working Instructions

Herringbone Stitch is a decorative border stitch. It is suitable for working in straight lines around other stitches, or along the edge of items such as tablecloths and napkins.

Begin by bringing the needle up at 1 and down at 2. Make a short, horizontal stitch to the left bringing the needle up at 3. Take the needle down to make a diagonal stitch at 4, then up again at 5.

Whipped Herringbone Stitch is an attractive alternative, especially if the whipping stitches are in a different colour. First complete a row of Herringbone Stitch, then use a blunt-ended needle to work whipping stitches without piercing the fabric.

BORDER STITCHES

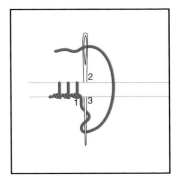

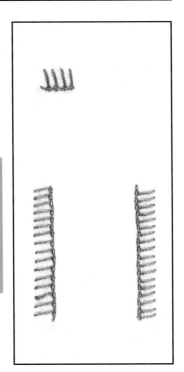

Working Instructions

Berwick Stitch has a similar appearance to Blanket Stitch but gives a more raised, knotted edge. It is useful as a border for other stitching or where a heavy outline is required. The vertical stitches must all be of the same length so it is advisable to draw two parallel lines on to your fabric as guidelines.

Bring the needle up on the lower line at 1, down at 2 and up again at 3, without pulling the needle all the way through the fabric. Twist the thread around the needle and pull tightly to form a neat knot. Draw the needle through slowly, holding the knot in place on the fabric. Continue working the line making sure that your stitches are evenly spaced.

Bonnet

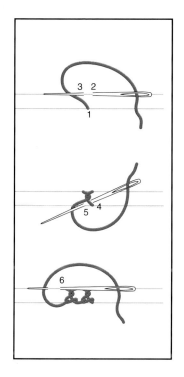

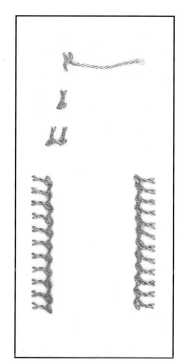

Working Instructions

Bonnet Stitch forms an intricate line. It is very good for decorative borders and works well on straight or gently curving lines – if it curves too sharply the effect is lost. The stitches must all be of the same length to give a neat appearance; guidelines drawn on the fabric will help you to achieve this.

Begin by bringing the needle up at 1, down at 2 and up at 3, keeping the thread under the needle. Push the needle under the stitch you have just made, down at 4 and up again at 5 with the thread under the needle. Start working the next stitch by pushing the needle back into the fabric on the top guideline at 6. This stitch is always worked form right to left.

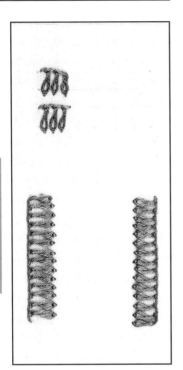

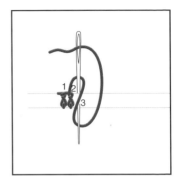

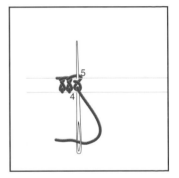

Working Instructions

Basque Stitch is an attractive border stitch which is worked in lines to give a pretty, looped edge. It also curves easily and looks particularly effective when worked in spirals. It is important to keep all the stitches the same length.

Bring the needle up at 1, down at 2, then up at 3, without pulling the needle all the way through the fabric. Next loop the thread around the needle as shown. Ease the needle through the fabric slowly, holding the loop in position as you pull. Make a small, vertical stitch at 4 just below the point where the thread emerges. Bring the needle up at 5 to start the next stitch.

Cross

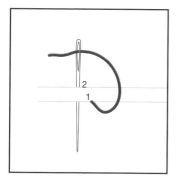

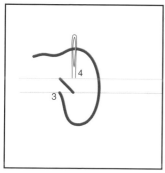

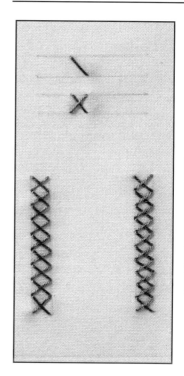

Working Instructions

Cross Stitch is one of the most common embroidery stitches. Each cross can be worked to any size, depending on the effect you wish to achieve. This stitch can be worked in horizontal or vertical rows with all the stitch points touching. It makes attractive borders or can be used to fill a shape. Cross Stitch is also useful as an isolated stitch worked at random over the fabric.

Bring the needle up at 1 and down at 2 to form a diagonal stitch. Bring the needle up again at 3, across the first stitch and down at 4. When working in rows the top diagonal stitches should all lie in the same direction.

Braid

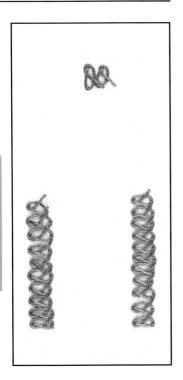

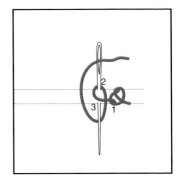

Working Instructions

Braid Stitch is an intricate stitch which requires a little practice. It forms an unusual and attractive line ideal for straight, decorative borders. However, the loops can easily become loose if it is used on an item that receives a lot of wear.

Bring the needle up at 1. Loop the thread around the needle, insert it back into the fabric on the top line at 2 and bring it up again at 3, without pulling the needle through the fabric. Pull the thread until the loop lies neatly on the fabric and hold it in place as you pull the needle through to the back. Work all the stitches close together in the same way, making sure that you pull the thread so that the loops are all the same size.

Loop

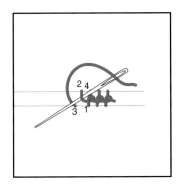

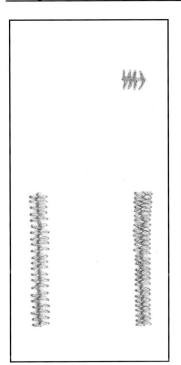

Working Instructions

Loop Stitch is an attractive stitch with a looped centre. The stitches can be made to any length, although the effect is more pronounced if you keep them short. Loop Stitch can be used as a border around other stitches, either in a straight line or a gentle curve. It can also be worked in close rows to fill a shape. Loop Stitch is particularly effective along the edge of a piece of fabric.

Bring the needle up between the guidelines at 1 and then down at 2, not pulling the thread too tightly. Bring the needle up again at 3 and take it under the first stitch at 4, keeping the thread under the needle. Continue working in this way making sure that the needle only pierces the fabric at the edges of the stitch.

BORDER STITCHES

Basket

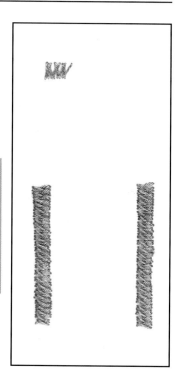

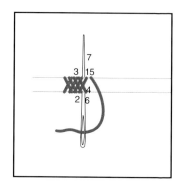

Working Instructions

Basket Stitch is an attractive border stitch. It can be worked closely to form a dense line or in a more open way to create an intricate, woven effect. Basket Stitch can also be stitched in rows to fill shapes. You will find stitching easier if you draw two parallel lines on to the fabric to guide you.

Begin by bringing the needle up at 1, then take it down at 2. Bring the needle up again on the top guideline at 3, then down at 4. Bring the needle up at 5, down between the last two stitches at 6, up at 7 and so on. Make sure that you space the stitches evenly, either close together or further apart depending on the effect you wish to create.

Roman

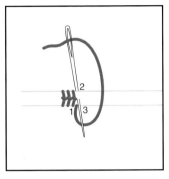

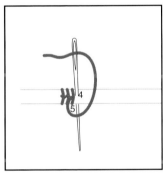

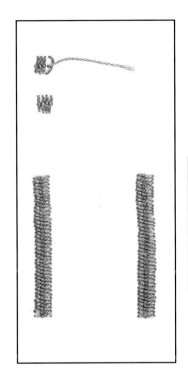

Working Instructions

Roman Stitch creates a broad, closely-worked line. It is best used for straight lines or gentle curves to maintain a dense coverage of the fabric. The stitches can be made to any length depending on the area you wish to fill. Roman Stitch makes an attractive border around other stitches and can be useful in pictorial work wherever you need a textured effect, such as stonework or tree trunks.

Bring the needle up at 1, down at 2, then up between the guidelines at 3, keeping the thread under the needle. Tie this stitch down with a short horizontal stitch at 4. Bring the needle up again at 5 to start the next stitch. Continue working in this way making sure that the short 'tying' stitches form a straight line.

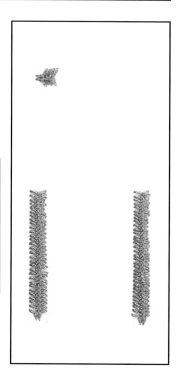

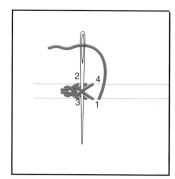

Working Instructions

Vandyke Stitch forms a raised, textured line which is simple but very effective. It is useful in pictorial work where a raised stitch is needed to depict unusual flower stems or branches. The length of the stitch can be adjusted to suit different designs and it can also be used as a border around other stitching.

This stitch lies on top of the fabric, piercing it only at the edges. Bring the needle up at 1, under the stitches at 2, up at 3 and down at 4. At first you will have to pick up a small piece of fabric between 2 and 3 but as you work further you should thread the needle under the last stitch. Work all the stitches close together making sure that the central ridge runs in a straight line.

Ladder

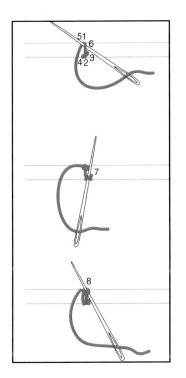

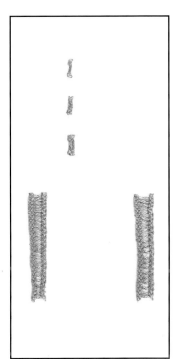

Working Instructions

Ladder Stitch is a most attractive and intricate embroidery stitch. It is best used for work that will have little wear as the raised edges may become flattened.

You will find this stitch easy to master with a little practice. Bring the needle up at 1 and down at 2 to make a straight vertical stitch, then up at 3 and down at 4 to form a small loop. Come up again at 5 and make another loop by taking the needle under the first straight stitch at 6. Make a second straight stitch and push the needle under the lower loop at 7 without piercing the fabric. Take the needle up to make a small stitch at 8. Continue working in this way looping the thread from side to side.

Rope

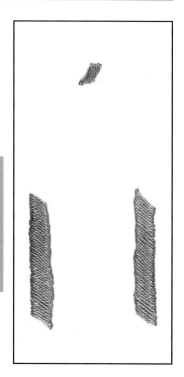

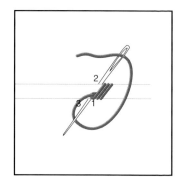

Working Instructions

Rope Stitch has a similar appearance to Satin Stitch but the addition of a knot gives it a more raised effect. This stitch gives a good coverage of the fabric. It can be worked in a straight line or the length of the stitches varied to fill different shapes. It is particularly good for making shapes stand out from the fabric; for instance, leaves look effective worked in two rows of Rope Stitch with the knotted edges touching to make a 'vein'.

Rope Stitch is worked from right to left. Bring the needle up at 1, down at 2 and up at 3, keeping the thread under the needle. Pull slowly to form a neat knot at the bottom of the stitch. The knots will be covered by subsequent stitches.

Feather

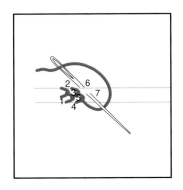

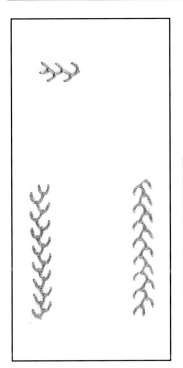

Working Instructions

Feather Stitch is a pretty, intricate stitch which is easy to learn. It is versatile enough to be worked in straight lines to add a border to other stitching, or in curved lines as detail in pictorial work. Feather Stitch may also be used in smocking to produce a very attractive effect.

Feather Stitch is formed from two small loops which interlock across the fabric. Bring the needle up at 1, down at 2 and up at 3, with the thread under the needle. Pull the needle through the fabric to make a loop. Make the next loop by pushing the needle down at 4 and up at 5, with the thread under the needle. Continue making these upper and lower loops alternately.

Double Feather

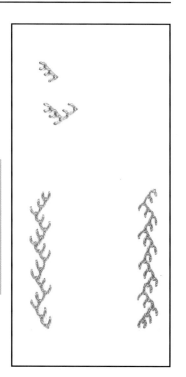

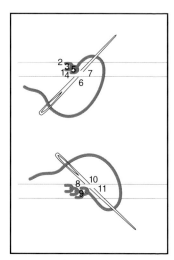

Working Instructions

Double Feather Stitch is worked in the same way as Feather Stitch but it is formed from three small loops instead of two. It is more intricate and delicate than Feather Stitch and makes a decorative, lacy edging.

Make the first loop by bringing the needle up at 1, down at 2 and up at 3, with the thread under the needle. Bring the needle up again at 4, down at 5 and up at 6 to form the second loop. Work three loops diagonally down the fabric then two loops up by bringing the needle up at 7, down at 8 and up again at 9. Make sure that all the loops are of the same size and lie within the area you wish to work.

Closed Feather

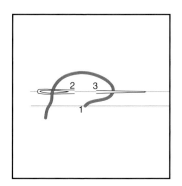

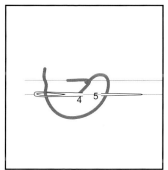

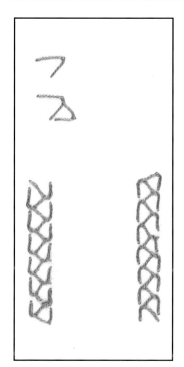

Working Instructions

Closed Feather Stitch is an enlarged version of Feather Stitch which is used mainly as a decorative border around other stitching. It can also be worked in a straight line as an attractive edging. As it is quite a wide stitch, you can achieve a more interesting effect by threading narrow ribbon between the stitches.

Bring the needle up on the lower line at 1, down at 2 on the upper line and up at 3, keeping the thread under the needle. Pull the needle through the fabric to form a loop. Push the needle down at 4 close to the first stitch, then up at 5 with the thread under the needle. Continue stitching in this way, working stitches on the upper and lower guidelines alternately.

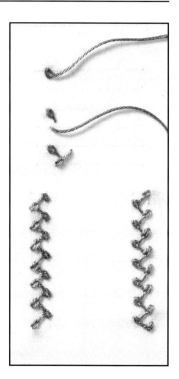

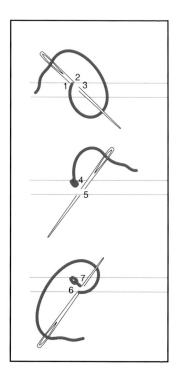

Working Instructions

Feathered Chain Stitch is one of the prettiest embroidery stitches. It creates a delicate, lacy effect which looks most effective when used to edge garments. It can also be used in pictorial work to add detail to items such as stems and flowers, or as a border for a whole design.

Begin by making a small chain 'link'. Bring the needle up at 1, down close by at 2 and up at 3, with the thread under the needle. Push the needle down again at 4 to secure the link with a short, diagonal stitch, then up at 5. Push the needle back down at 6 and up at 7 to make the next link. Continue working links which slant in opposite directions from the upper line to the lower line.

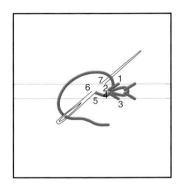

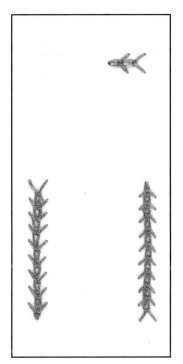

Working Instructions

Wheatear Chain Stitch is a decorative stitch which makes an attractive border. It can be worked along the edge of garments or used in pictorial work where it is effective for working ears of wheat, as its name suggests.

Bring the needle up at 1, down at 2, up at 3 and down at 4 to make two diagonal stitches which touch at the centre. Bring the needle up at 5, thread it through the two diagonal stitches and push it down again at 6, next to where the thread emerged. Bring the needle up again at 7 to begin working the next diagonal stitch. Continue in this way, completing two diagonal stitches and a Chain Stitch alternately.

Open Chain

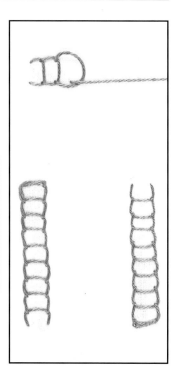

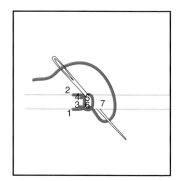

Working Instructions

Open Chain Stitch is also known as Square Chain Stitch as it creates a pattern of square chain links across the fabric. It is particularly effective when used as an edging on garments or table linen. Alternatively, it can be used as a wide filling or for larger details in pictorial work.

Open Chain Stitch is worked by bringing the needle up at 1, down at 2 and up at 3, keeping the thread under the needle. Pull the thread through the fabric slowly to form a loop. Each square chain link is held in place by the next. When you come to the end of your line of stitching, work a small stitch over the edge of the last chain link to secure it.

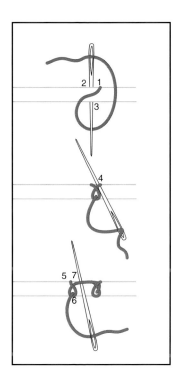

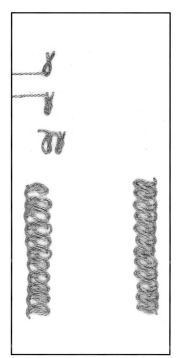

BORDER STITCHES

Working Instructions

Rosette Chain Stitch forms an intricate, looped line which is easy to master with a little practice. It is designed to be a raised stitch, so it is only suitable for items which will have little wear. It is best used to add detail to pictorial work or as a decorative filling.

Bring the needle up at 1, down at 2 and up at 3 with the thread taken across the fabric and under the needle. Pull the needle slowly through the fabric to form a twisted loop, then push the needle under the top of the loop at 4 without piercing the fabric. Take the needle across to 5 and up at 6, twisting the needle around the thread as before. Bring the needle under the thread at 7 to start the next stitch.

Filling Stitches

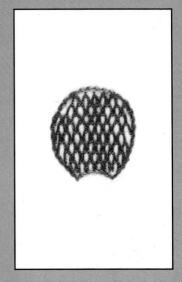

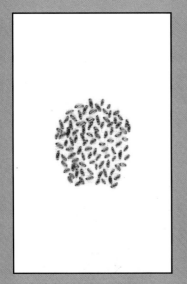

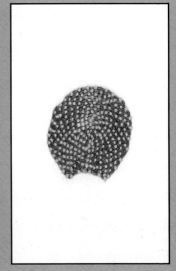

Satin

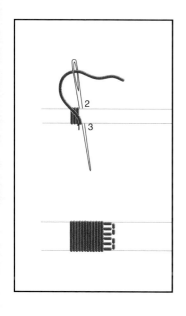

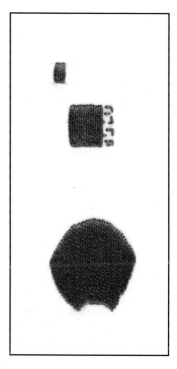

Working Instructions

Satin Stitch is one of the most popular filling stitches as it covers the fabric well with a smooth, even surface. It is versatile enough to be graduated to fit any size of area.

Work with an embroidery hoop to keep the tension of the stitches even. Bring the needle up at 1, down at 2 and up again at 3. Keep stitching in this under and over motion so that the back of the work looks the same as the front.

Padded Satin Stitch gives a more raised appearance. Fill an area with stitches – Running, Chain or Backstitches – and then work Satin Stitch over the top. Our example is padded with Running Stitch.

Flat

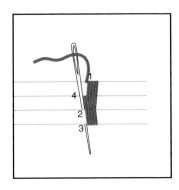

Working Instructions

Flat Stitch is a very useful embroidery stitch. It covers an area quite quickly and looks particularly effective when used to fill leaf or petal shapes as it creates a central ridge.

It is important to maintain an even tension when working Flat Stitch as the stitches should all lie close together to produce a smooth surface. You will find it easier to work if you draw two parallel lines along the centre of the shape to use as guidelines for the slanted stitches.

Begin by bringing the needle up at 1 and down at 2 to make the first slanted stitch. Bring the needle up again at 3 to start the next stitch and push it back down at 4 to complete.

Fishbone

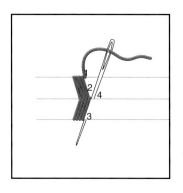

Working Instructions

Fishbone Stitch is worked in the same way as Flat Stitch but the stitches are worked at a sharper angle and cross over directly at the centre. Fishbone Stitch covers the fabric completely and is particularly effective where a pronounced centre line is required.

It is best to work with an embroidery hoop and to draw a guideline along the centre of the shape to keep the stitches uniform. You can graduate the stitches to fill a shape but the crossing points should always form a straight line. Bring the needle up at 1 and down at 2 to form a slanted stitch. Bring the needle up again at 3 to begin the next slanted stitch, and down at 4 to complete. Continue working in this way to fill the shape.

Long & Short

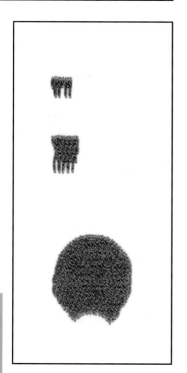

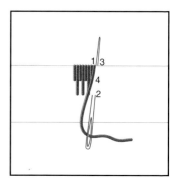

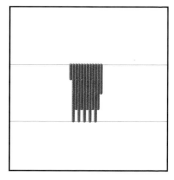

Working Instructions

Long and Short Stitch is a very versatile stitch which creates an attractive, textured appearance. It works particularly well where subtle shading is required.

Work alternate long and short stitches for the first row – the short stitches should be half the length of the long stitches. Bring the needle up at 1, down at 2, up at 3, down at 4 and so on. Subsequent rows are worked with the stitches all the same length, equal to the long stitches in the first row. It is important to work the stitches close together so that all the background fabric is covered. When you reach the final row, finish the block with long and short stitches in the same way as you worked the first row.

Roumanian

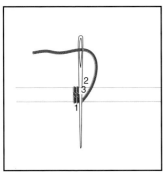

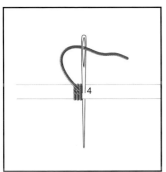

Working Instructions

Roumanian Stitch is an attractive stitch which produces a neat, raised strip down the centre of your work. It is very useful in pictorial work as the length of the stitches can be graduated to fill any shape. It is particularly effective for abstract work or pictorial designs which require a raised central strip.

Bring the needle up at 1, down at 2 and up again at 3 midway between these two points – the thread should emerge to the left of the stitch just made. Take the thread over the stitch and push the needle down at 4 to make a short, slanted stitch. Graduate the length of the long stitches to fit the desired shape but keep all the central stitches the same length and in a straight line.

Cretan

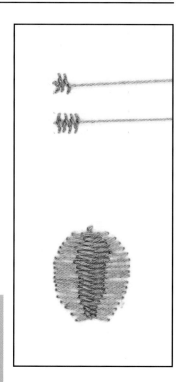

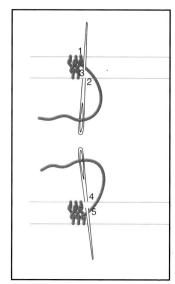

Working Instructions

Cretan Stitch is an attractive stitch which is particularly useful for wide borders. As its name suggests, it originated in Crete where it was traditionally used to decorate items such as table linen. Cretan Stitch can also be used in pictorial work for filling shapes such as leaves as it creates a central 'vein'. It can be worked with the stitches spaced apart, as in this example, or close together so that the background fabric cannot be seen.

Begin by bringing the needle up at 1, down at 2 and up at 3, holding the thread under the needle to form a loop. Bring the needle up again at 4 and down at 5 to form another loop. Continue filling the area by making upper and lower loops alternately.

Laid Work

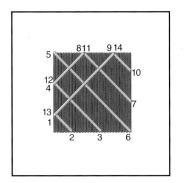

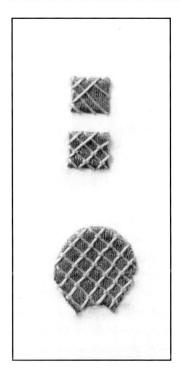

Working Instructions

Laid Work is a raised filling stitch which can be adapted to cover any area. It is often found in abstract designs or in pictorial work, especially crewel work.

First fill the area with Satin Stitches, making sure that they are worked closely enough to cover the background fabric. Work the laid stitches on top by bringing the needle up at 1, down at 2, up at 3, down at 4 and so on. Next work diagonal stitches in the opposite direction by bringing the needle up at 11, down at 12 and so on. Make sure that the ends of the second set of diagonal stitches touch the ends of the first set. To finish, work small stitches over each intersection to hold the threads in place.

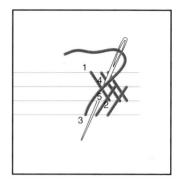

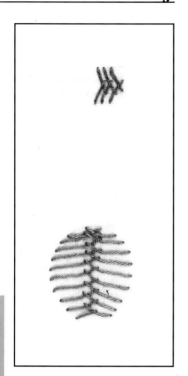

Working Instructions

Leaf Stitch is an open stitch which can be used for filling any shape. As the name suggests, it is good for filling leaf shapes as the effect of a 'vein' is created. It can also be worked between parallel lines to form a border around other stitching.

It is easier to work Leaf Stitch if you draw two parallel guidelines through the centre of the shape to be filled. Bring the needle up at 1, then down at 2 on the lower guideline. Bring the needle up again at 3, down at 4 and up at 5, with the needle under the thread. Push the needle down at 6 to complete the two diagonal stitches. Continue in this way making sure that the diagonal stitches slope alternately and are evenly spaced.

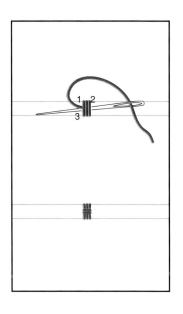

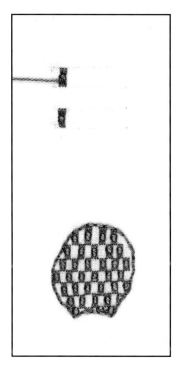

Working Instructions

Sheaf Stitch is useful wherever a small, raised block of stitches is required. Also known as Sheaf Filling, it can be used alone or in groups to fill an area.

If you want to use Sheaf Stitch as a filling stitch, you must take care to space the sheaves an equal distance apart. Begin by making three vertical stitches close together. Bring the needle up to the left of these stitches at 1. Take the thread over the stitches and push it under them at 2, bringing it out at 3 without piercing the fabric. Work another of these 'tying' stitches and insert the needle back into the fabric to complete. Pull tight enough to create a sheaf effect but take care not to pucker the fabric.

FILLING STITCHES

Basket Filling

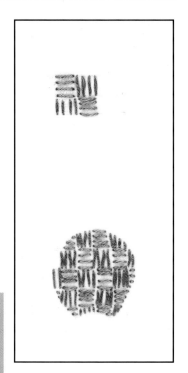

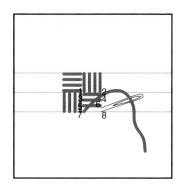

Working Instructions

Basket Filling Stitch is an attractive embroidery stitch which is
ideal for working textured areas, such as walls, roofs and
stonework. It can be worked quite quickly and can be graduated
easily to fill any shape. If you work on a plain weave fabric, you
must take care to keep the groups of stitches in straight lines. This
stitch can also be worked on an evenweave fabric using the holes
to guide you.

Work the stitches horizontally and vertically in groups of four.
To achieve a uniform appearance you must make sure that the
individual stitches and the groups of four are evenly spaced. Bring
the needle up at 1, down at 2, up at 3, down at 4 and so on.

Chevron

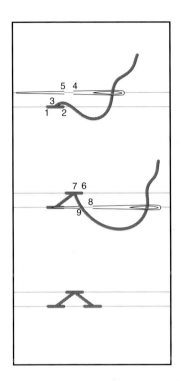

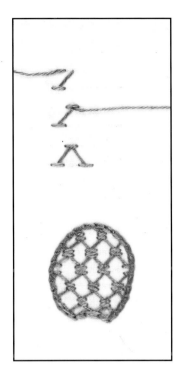

Working Instructions

Chevron Stitch is a versatile embroidery stitch which can be used for filling shapes or for working borders. It is often used as a decorative stitch in smocking, worked across the fabric pleats.

Begin by bringing the needle up at 1, down at 2 and up again in the centre of the stitch at 3. Make another small stitch by taking the needle down at 4 and up at 5. Push the needle down at 6 then up again at 7. Take the needle down at 8 and up at 9 to start the next horizontal stitch. You will find it easier to make the horizontal stitches if you leave the thread slightly loose while you bring the needle through at the centre, then tighten it. Make sure that you keep the stitches an equal distance apart.

Arrowhead

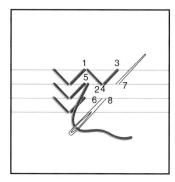

Working Instructions

Arrowhead Stitch is an open filling stitch which can be worked on both plain weave and evenweave fabrics. It can be used to fill any shape but is most effective in straight areas. It forms an attractive, zig-zag line useful for abstract work and individual stitches can also be worked randomly.

Arrowhead Stitch is worked by stitching a pair of diagonal lines to form a 'V' shape. Bring the needle up at 1 and down at 2 to make the first stitch, then up at 3 and down at 4 to make the second. Continue in rows making sure that the point of each new stitch touches the last. It is important to keep all the stitches the same length to achieve a uniform appearance.

Buttonhole Filling

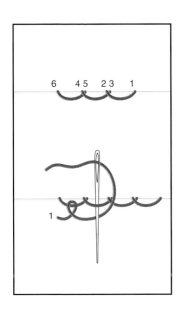

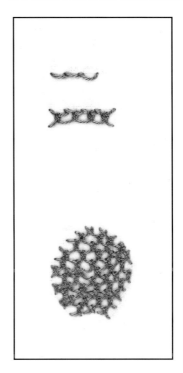

Working Instructions

Buttonhole Filling is a detached filling stitch which only passes through the fabric at the edge of the design. This lacy stitch should be used on work that will have very little wear, as the effect may be lost if the loops are disturbed.

Work the first row in the sequence shown. Subsequent rows are all worked on the surface except for the edges. Bring the needle up at 1, then through the stitch above, with the thread kept under the needle, to form a small loop. Finish off by pushing the needle back into the fabric before bringing it up again to start the next row. Always work from left to right then right to left and so on. Finally, catch down the loops with small stitches into the fabric.

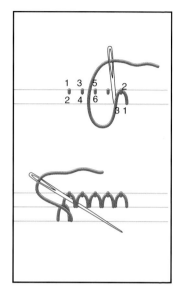

Working Instructions

Wave Stitch is an open filling stitch made up of interwoven loops. It is most effective where a decorative, lacy effect is required.

Start by working a line of short, vertical stitches. These stitches will anchor the first set of loops. Bring the needle up at 1, down at 2, up at 3, down at 4 and so on. To work the first row of loops bring the needle up at 1, through the anchoring stitch at 2, without piercing the fabric, then down at 3.

For subsequent rows, thread the needle through the base of two loops in the previous row as shown. It is important to work the base of the loops close together so that the thread of the next row can be worked through them.

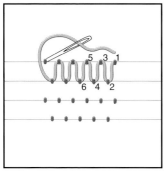

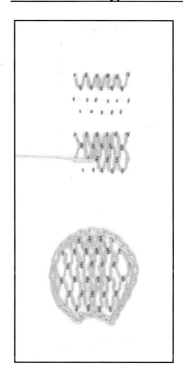

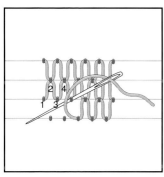

Working Instructions

Cloud Filling Stitch is used mainly as a decorative stitch in pictorial work, and on garments and table linen.

Start by working a row of short, evenly-spaced stitches. When you have filled the area, weave another thread in and out of the stitches without piercing the fabric. Bring the needle up at 1, through at 2, through at 3 and so on. Push the needle back into the fabric when you reach the end of the row. Begin the next row by bringing the thread up at the bottom straight stitch at 1, then under the stitch at 2, sharing it with the loop in the previous row and so on. Continue in this way making sure that you begin each row alternately at the top and then bottom straight stitches.

FILLING STITCHES

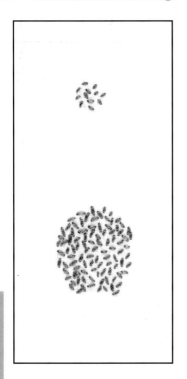

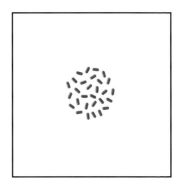

Working Instructions

Seeding is a very versatile stitch which is made up of short stitches worked randomly in different directions. Seeding can be used to fill any area and creates a light, delicate filling. It is useful for pictorial work such as landscapes. If you use several tones of the same colour a delicate, shaded effect can be achieved.

Seeding is easy to work as there is no particular pattern to follow, but the stitches should all be of the same length and evenly spaced. You should not aim for a uniform appearance but, as the name suggests, scatter the stitches across the fabric as if throwing seeds on the ground.

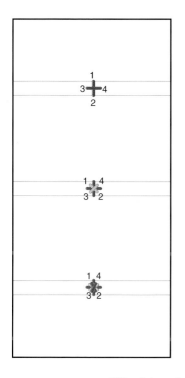

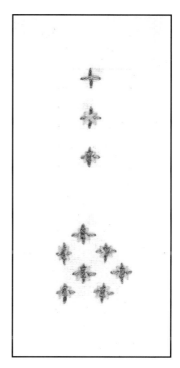

Working Instructions

Star Filling Stitch is made up of three layers of crosses worked on top of each other. It can be used as an isolated stitch, worked in straight rows of evenly-spaced stars, or with the stars scattered across the fabric for an unusual, abstract effect.

The first stage is to stitch an upright cross. Bring the needle up at 1, down at 2, up at 3 and down at 4. The next cross is worked diagonally across the first by bringing the needle up at 1, down at 2, up at 3 and down at 4. Finally, work a small, elongated cross over the fist two by bringing the needle up at 1, down at 2, up at 3 and down at 4. All three crosses can be the same colour or each layer can be different for a more dramatic effect.

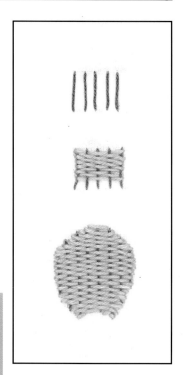

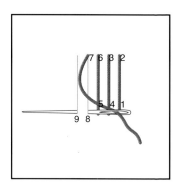

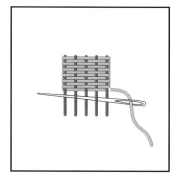

Working Instructions

Weaving Stitch gives a good coverage of the fabric and is easy to work. It works well to represent stonework, fences and baskets.

This stitch is worked in two stages. First complete a row of evenly-spaced, vertical stitches by bringing the needle up at 1, down at 2, up at 3, down at 4 and so on. To work the weaving, bring the needle up at one side of the straight stitches. Weave the thread under and over the straight stitches and push the needle back into the fabric at the far side. Bring it up again a little lower down and weave another row of stitches directly below the first. The thread should go under the stitches it went over in the previous row and vice versa. Continue working in this way.

Plaited

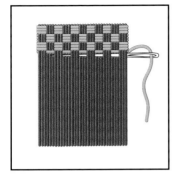

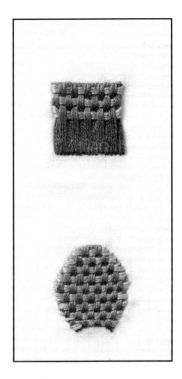

Working Instructions

Plaited Stitch is a very attractive stitch which looks best when the weaving and straight stitches are worked in a different colours.

Begin by working a dense group of straight stitches. Bring the needle up at at the top of the area, down at the bottom, up next to the last stitch, back up to the top of the area, and so on. Work the weaving stitches by taking the needle over three stitches, then under three, over three and so on. Push the needle into the fabric just beyond the last straight stitch and bring it back up just below. Work the second and third rows in this way. For the fourth row, weave the thread under the three stitches which you worked over previously and vice versa. Continue working blocks in this way.

Couching

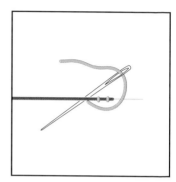

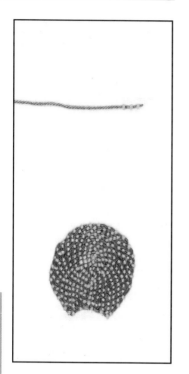

Working Instructions

Couching involves laying a thread across the fabric and securing it with a series of small stitches. Couching is often used in goldwork to hold down thick, metallic threads.

Bring the laid thread up at the edge of the design line. Bring the couching thread up just beyond this. Manipulate the laid thread into position and work small, vertical stitches over it. Each of these 'couching' stitches should be the same width as the laid thread and worked at equal intervals along it. When you reach the end of the design line, take the laid thread to the back of the fabric then the couching thread. When you work around curves you will need to make the couching stitches closer together.

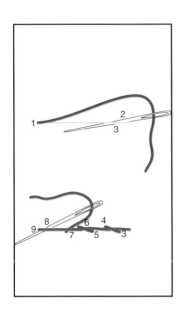

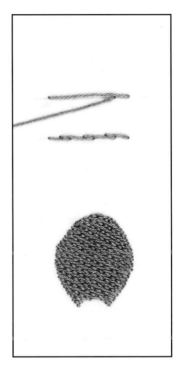

Working Instructions

Roumanian Couching can be used to outline a shape or to fill an area, providing that the couching lines are worked close together. It differs from basic couching as the same thread is used for both the laying and securing stitches.

Roumanian Couching is worked by bringing the needle up at 1 and down at 2. Bring the needle up again at 3, making sure that the thread lies flat on the fabric and is not pulled too tight. Take the needle over the laid thread at 4 to make a slanted stitch, then up at 5, down at 6, up at 7, down at 8 and up at 9. The slanted stitches should all be of the same length and evenly spaced to achieve a uniform appearance.

Jacobean Couching

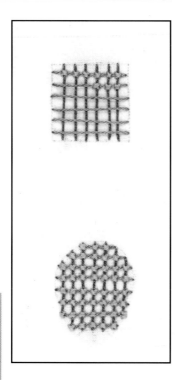

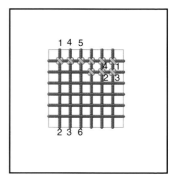

Working Instructions

Jacobean Couching is an attractive stitch which is more striking if worked in two colours. Also known as Trellis Work, it is traditionally found in Jacobean embroidery and looks particularly effective when used to fill flower centres.

Start by working a set of evenly-spaced, vertical stitches. Bring the needle up at 1, down at 2, up at 3, down at 4 and so on. For the next stage, work horizontal stitches over the vertical ones to form a grid. Finally, fasten down the straight stitches with a small cross at all the points where the vertical and horizontal stitches intersect. Bring the needle up at 1, down at 2, up at 3 and down at 4 to form each cross.

Knots/Isolated Stitches

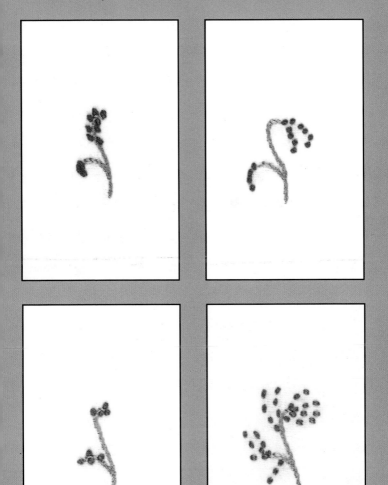

French Knot

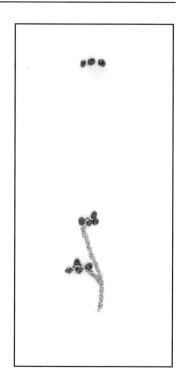

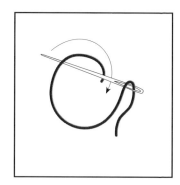

Working Instructions

French Knots are the most common type of embroidered knot. They can be used singly for small details, such as eyes, or in closely-worked groups for features such as flower centres. You can stitch these knots in just one colour or create a different look by combining two colours of thread in your needle.

Holding the thread with your left hand, twist the needle around the thread twice (do not twist the thread around the needle). Insert the point of the needle back into the fabric and pull the thread to tighten the knot. Push the needle through the fabric close to where the thread emerged. You can make a larger knot by increasing the number of times you twist the needle.

Danish Knot

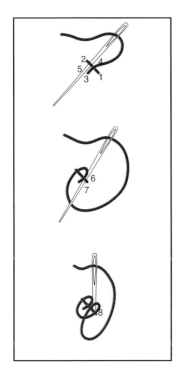

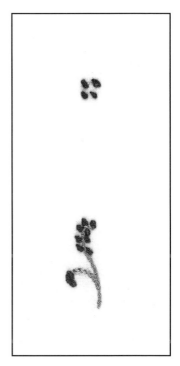

Working Instructions

Danish Knots can be used instead of French Knots but they have a squarer appearance. They can be used singly for small details, or in clusters to fill an area of the fabric.

To begin, bring the needle up at 1, then down at 2 to form a diagonal stitch. Bring the needle up at 3 and thread it under the diagonal stitch at 4 and out the other side at 5. Repeat this twisting motion by taking the needle back under the other side of the stitch at 6 and out again at 7. To finish the Danish Knot, take the thread over to 8 and through to the back of the fabric.

Colonial Knot

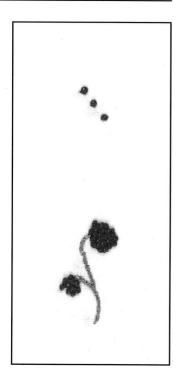 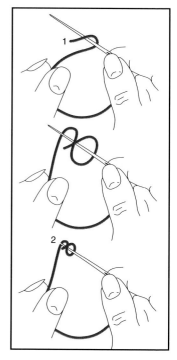

Working Instructions

Colonial Knots have a raised, textured appearance which is easy to achieve with a little practice. They can be used individually or worked in clusters to fill an area of the fabric. These knots are traditionally used in Candlewick Embroidery where a thick thread is worked into large, raised knots.

Bring the needle up at 1 and loop the thread over it. Next take the thread over and under the needle in a figure of eight. Push the needle back down into the fabric at 2, close to where it first emerged. Before you pull it all the way through, tighten the loops around the needle and hold them in place on the fabric. Pull the needle through carefully to form a neat knot.

Chinese Knot

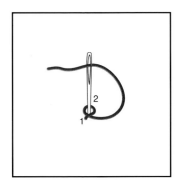

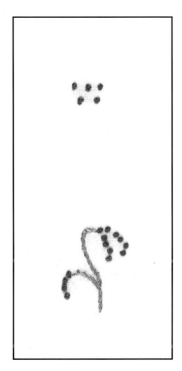

Working Instructions

Chinese Knots are flat with a slight dip in the centre. They are very effective used singly in pictorial designs but can also be worked in a curved line to give an effect such as blossom on trees. Alternatively, Chinese Knots can be worked close together to fill areas where a raised, textured appearance is required.

This is a very quick and easy knot to work. Bring the thread up through the fabric at 1. Loop the thread around the needle, then insert the needle back into the fabric close to where it first emerged but do not pull it all the way through. Tighten the loop around the needle and hold it in place on the fabric. Secure the knot by pulling the needle through to the back of the fabric.

Bullion Knot

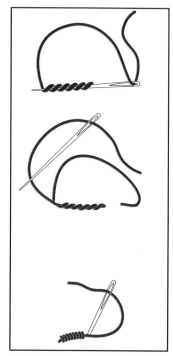

Working Instructions

Bullion Knots take a little practice but it is worth persevering.
This striking three-dimensional stitch can be worked to any length
and even made into rings. It is important to use a fine needle.

Bring the needle up through the fabric and insert it a short
distance away to set the length of the stitch. Bring it up again at
the point where the thread first emerged but don't pull the needle
all the way through. Wrap the thread around the tip of the needle
as many times as the stitch length requires. Holding the twists
firmly with your thumb, pull the needle up through both the fabric
and the coil of thread. Pull back in the opposite direction so that
the coil lies flat on the fabric. Take the needle through to the back.

Straight

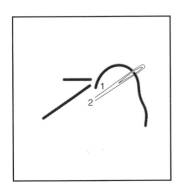

Working Instructions

Straight Stitch is a very versatile embroidery stitch as it can be worked to any length and in any direction. It is particularly useful in pictorial work for adding details such as flower stems and branches. If you work Straight Stitch in different directions and to different lengths, a realistic grassy effect can be achieved. It can also be used to outline other areas of stitching providing that the edges are straight.

Straight Stitch is very simple to work; bring the needle up at 1 and then down again at 2 to give the required length of stitch.

Lazy Daisy

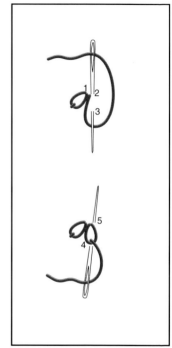

Working Instructions

Lazy Daisy Stitch is also known as Detached Chain Stitch as each stitch is formed from an individual chain 'link'. It is a very popular embroidery stitch used on both plain weave and evenweave fabrics. As its name suggests, it is most commonly used to represent flowers but the stitches may also be used individually to decorate other work.

Bring the needle up at 1 and down at 2, without pulling the needle all the way through the fabric. Bring it up again at 3, with the thread under the needle, and pull gently to form a loop. Secure the loop by pushing the needle into the fabric at 4. If you wish to make another stitch next to it, repeat this method starting at 5.

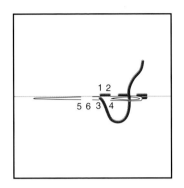

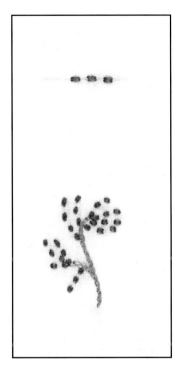

Working Instructions

Dot Stitch is a very pretty embroidery stitch. Its appearance is similar to Seeding but two short, straight stitches are used instead of one. Worked singly or in groups, this stitch is most effective in pictorial work as it can be used to depict items such as flowers or seed heads. Dot Stitch can also be worked in close rows to give a 'peppered' effect, or even to outline other stitches.

Begin by bringing the needle up at 1, down at 2, up next to the first stitch at 3, then down again at 4. Leave a small space before bringing the needle up again at 5, down at 6 and so on.

Spiders Web

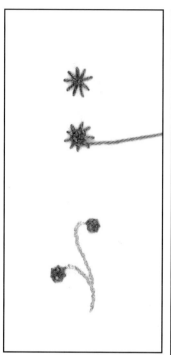
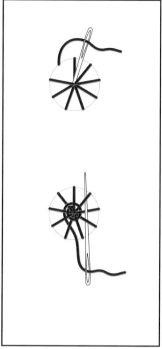

Working Instructions

Spider's Web is an easy stitch to work, yet it gives an unusual effect. It can all be completed in the same colour, or the straight and weaving stitches can be worked in contrasting colours. It is easier to stitch if you draw a circle on to the fabric to the required size of the 'web'.

Begin by working the straight stitches. Use an odd number of stitches (there are nine in this example) so that you finish in the centre of the circle. Bring a new thread up in the centre of the circle and weave it under and over the straight stitches until you have filled the 'web' right up to the end of the straight stitches. Take the needle through to the back of the fabric to finish.

Index